MEDICAL PRACTICE MANAGEMENT
Body of Knowledge Review

VOLUME 2

Business and Clinical Operations

Edward Gulko, MBA, FACMPE, CHE

Managing Editor
Lawrence F. Wolper, MBA, FACMPE

Medical Group
Management
Association

Medical Group Management Association
104 Inverness Terrace East
Englewood, CO 80112-5306
877.275.6462
Website: www.mgma.com

Medical Group Management Association (MGMA) publications are intended to provide current and accurate information and are designed to assist readers in becoming more familiar with the subject matter covered. Such publications are distributed with the understanding that MGMA does not render any legal, accounting, or other professional advice that may be construed as specifically applicable to an individual situation. No representations or warranties are made concerning the application of legal or other principles discussed by the authors to any specific factual situation, nor is any prediction made concerning how any particular judge, government official, or other person will interpret or apply such principles. Specific factual situations should be discussed with professional advisors.

Production Credits
Executive Editor: Andrea M. Rossiter, FACMPE
Managing Editor: Lawrence F. Wolper, MBA, FACMPE
Editorial Director: Marilee E. Aust
Production Editor: Marti A. Cox, MLIS
Page Design, Composition and Production: Boulder Bookworks
Substantive and Copy Editor: Sandra Rush, Rush Services
Proofreader: Scott Vickers, InstEdit
Cover Design: Ian Serff, Serff Creative Group, Inc.
MGMA Editorial Council Reviewer: Ruth L. Lander, FACMPE
MGMA and ACMPE Member Reviewer: Marianne Spurgeon, RN, BSN

PUBLISHER'S CATALOGING IN PUBLICATION DATA

Gulko, Edward.
    Business and clinical operations / by Edward Gulko ; managing editor Lawrence F. Wolper. – Englewood, CO : MGMA, 2006.
    82 p. : 3 ill. ; cm. – (Medical Practice Management Body of Knowledge Review Series ; v. 2)
Includes index.
ISBN 1-56829-241-4
    1. Group practice management. 2. Practice management, Medical. [MeSH] 3. Group medical practice. [LC] 4. Medical offices—Management. [LC] I. Wolper, Lawrence F. II. Medical Group Management Association. III. American College of Medical Practice Executives. IV. Series. V. Series: Body of Knowledge Review Series.

R729.5.G85 2006
658.042—dc22   2005938793

Item 6361

ISBN: 1-56829-241-4   Library of Congress Control Number: 2005938793

Printed in the United States of America
10 9 8 7 6 5 4 3 2 1

Acknowledgments

I would like to thank Edward Ludwig, FACMPE, for his help in reviewing the manuscript for accuracy and completeness; my administrative assistant Linda Tarantino, for her help in proofreading; and Marilee Aust, MGMA, for keeping me on the right track.

Most important, I want to thank my wife, Judy, for her understanding, support, and patience during this process.

Contents

Series Overview

THE MEDICAL GROUP MANAGEMENT ASSOCIATION (MGMA) serves medical practices of all sizes, as well as management services organizations, integrated delivery systems, and ambulatory surgery centers to assist members with information, education, networking, and advocacy. Through the American College of Medical Practice Executives® (ACMPE®), MGMA's standard-setting and certification body, the organization provides board certification and Fellowship in medical practice management and supports those seeking to advance their careers.

■ Core Learning Series: A professional development pathway for competency and excellence in medical practice management

Medical practice management is one of the fastest-growing and most rewarding careers in health care administration. It is also one of the most demanding, requiring a breadth of skills and knowledge unique to the group practice environment. For these reasons, MGMA and ACMPE have created a comprehensive series of learning resources, customized to meet the specific professional development needs of medical practice managers: the *Medical Practice Management Core Learning Series*.

The Medical Practice Management Core Learning Series is a structured approach that enables practice administrators and staff to build the core knowledge and skills required for career success. Series resources include seminars, Web-based education programs, books, and online assessment tools. These resources provide a strong, expansive foundation for managing myriad job responsibilities and daily challenges.

■ Core Learning Series: Resources for understanding medical practice operations

To gain a firm footing in medical practice management, executives need a broad understanding of the knowledge and skills required to do the job. The Medical Practice Management Core Learning Series offers "Level 1" resources, which provide an introduction to the essentials of medical practice management. As part of the learning process, professionals can use these resources to assess their current level of knowledge across all competency areas, identify gaps in their education or experience, and select areas in which to focus further study. The *Medical Practice Management Body of Knowledge Review Series* is considered to be a Core Learning Series – Level 1 resource.

Level 1 resources meet the professional development needs of individuals who are new to or considering a career in the field of medical practice management, assuming practice management responsibilities, or considering ACMPE board certification in medical practice management.

Also offered are Core Learning Series – Level 2 resources, which provide exposure to more advanced concepts in specific competency areas and their application to day-to-day operation of the medical practice. These resources meet the needs of individuals who have more experience in the field, who seek specialized knowledge in a particular area of medical practice management, and/or who are completing preparations for the ACMPE board certification examinations.

■ Core Learning Series: Resources to become board certified

Board certification and Fellowship in ACMPE are well-earned badges of professional achievement. The designations Certified Medical Practice Executive (CMPE) and Fellow in ACMPE (FACMPE) indicate that the professional has attained significant levels of expertise across the full range of the medical practice administrator's responsibilities. The Medical Practice Management Core Learning Series is MGMA's recommended learning system for certification preparation. With attainment of the CMPE designation, practice executives will be well positioned to excel in their careers through ACMPE Fellowship.

Preface

TO SUCCEED AND FLOURISH in the day-to-day work environment of managing a medical practice, it is important that the successful administrator master and become adept at utilizing basic and advanced business and clinical operations skills.

The Business and Clinical Operations domain within the *ACMPE Guide to the Body of Knowledge for Medical Practice Management* presents the basic building blocks needed to efficiently and effectively manage the day-to-day operations of a medical group practice, regardless of its legal or political structure. Included within the general competency of Technical/Professional Knowledge and Skills, the Business and Clinical Operations domain requires an in-depth understanding of the other competencies for the effective management of a group practice.

When faced with the task of assuming the leadership of a medical practice, the effective medical practice executive should properly utilize the basic tools of business and clinical operations to properly evaluate the issues affecting the organization. Through the proper application of these tools, the administrator will be able to prepare and implement the steps needed to place the organization on a firm footing for survival and growth. Examples of the organizational effects that result when these tools are put to proper use can be seen in many organizations and real life experiences.

Knowledge of the tools within the business and clinical operations domain and the way they interact with the other domains within the *Guide* affords the health care administrator the ability to provide the direction and leadership needed by his or her organization. These same tools are utilized in the day-to-day operation of a practice and assist the administrator in assuring the continued growth and development of the organization.

Learning Objectives

AFTER READING THIS VOLUME, the medical practice executive will be able to:

1. Identify and explain the various roles staff and physicians play within a group practice;

2. Evaluate staffing needs and expectations;

3. Determine and document the clinical needs of a practice and identify complementary clinical opportunities and expectations;

4. Identify primary areas of cost control within a practice;

5. List the steps needed to identify and develop a proper facility that supports the needs of the organization and meets regulatory requirements;

6. Identify and list the "nuts-and-bolts" requirements of both the business and clinical aspects of a practice;

7. Understand the interplay and options for internal and external communications; and

8. Identify the methods and tools for evaluating the present and planning for the future.

CASE STUDY **ABC Medical Associates**

ABC MEDICAL ASSOCIATES in Maintown, N.H., had been in operation for more than 30 years and recently employed a succession of several administrators. The practice was experiencing numerous operational and financial problems that were jeopardizing its future viability. The organization had suffered significant financial losses in the previous year, physician income was down, staff morale was low, and there was increased documentation of patient dissatisfaction.

Herbert Bradford, FACMPE, Fellow of the American College of Medical Practice Executives, was hired as a new administrator with the charge to "save" ABC Medical Associates. In reviewing the organizational structure, Herb found that there were no written policies, no reviews of staffing patterns, no staff evaluations, no financial controls or timely reports, and no budgets in place. In addition, responses to patient complaints were not conducted on a timely basis and there were significant delays in posting charges and payments.

Herb addressed all of these issues within the first nine months of becoming an administrator, and within one year, policies were in place, morale had risen, all postings were done on a timely basis, and patient complaints had dropped significantly. As a final point, although some small "paper" financial losses continued to exist, the cash losses had been eliminated.

Business and clinical operations are truly at the heart (and in the soul) of every successful medical practice and its executives.

Business and Clinical Operations and the General Competencies

THE BUSINESS AND CLINICAL OPERATIONS domain requires all five general competencies to be in place for a medical practice executive to be successful.

■ Professionalism

The general competency of Professionalism is imperative to any business setting, but it is particularly important when clinical operations are added to the mix. A medical practice requires a constant flow of personal and confidential medical information and financial data – from patients, payers, and physicians – to successfully perform appropriate services. This information helps to set the foundation from which a patient can receive proper care. A core set of procedures, policies, and practices is necessary to position the framework from which the staff can work. The professionalism of how that information is managed, administered, and carried out sets the culture of the medical practice.

A medical practice can have the best set of business policies and procedures, but if these aren't administered and managed professionally, the integrity of the medical practice may suffer a loss of integrity and a lack of respect from its colleagues, which can translate into a loss of referrals. Professionalism should be a core organizational value for all medical practices, woven into the fabric of its daily life. This commitment to professional standards allows the organization to carry out its business in the most effective manner.

■ Leadership

Leadership can be defined as the ability to influence others. One is not capable of being an effective leader without integrity, trustworthiness, and high ethics. The Business and Clinical Operations domain requires the medical practice executive to lead an environment that fosters teamwork, accountability, and cooperation. It means that physicians should work hard to foster excellence through governance, education, training, and problem solving. In addition, the leadership of the practice must support the organization toward its mission, vision, and values. The trait of leadership is essential for the medical practice executive in the development of relationships for the business of medicine – as seen through the eyes of physicians, staff, patients, payers, and the surrounding community.

■ Communication Skills

Communication involves the art and science of expressing and exchanging ideas in speech or writing. The intricacies of life require that the medical practice executive master both oral and written communication skills. In the Business and Clinical Operations domain, communication is key to all parties, whether delivering the message or receiving it. It is not uncommon for an operational message to be misinterpreted or misunderstood due to a lack of clear communication skills. A challenge for many business professionals is how to identify the most appropriate communication media for the target audience. A further challenge is to support whatever dialogue needs to occur to answer questions, seek clarity, and resolve (and minimize) conflict.

■ Organizational and Analytical Skills

Tremendous amounts of data are needed to ensure that the Business and Clinical Operations domain is appropriately managed. Whether it is determining budgeting/forecasting models, establishing benchmarks, developing clinical pathways, or negotiating and evaluating third-party contracts, this domain demands an orientation and mastery of organizational and analytical skills.

Most financial statements are ultimately broken down to revenues vs. expenses, and many discussions are held over reimbursement rates or the lack thereof. Knowing how to manage this common concern requires an orientation to collecting and analyzing relevant information from multiple sources, discerning the salient data, and making sound decisions based on this information.

The Business and Clinical Operations domain requires the practice executive to interact with people, but communication cannot be effective without solid organizational/analytical skills. These skills help the executive to manage practice resources and work toward reaching consensus and achieving best performance.

■ Technical/Professional Knowledge and Skills

Operating a medical practice is not like managing a hospital, nursing home, or retail store. It requires a special set of technical and professional knowledge and skills unheard-of by other professions. The diversity and variety of situations that occur in a medical practice make its managers a unique breed. The medical practice executive is expected to have both a general knowledge of many areas as well as a specific capacity to handle detailed information in many areas. An example is the practice executive facilitating a physician-owner board meeting. In that meeting, the group will:

1. Review the monthly and year-to-date financials and budgets (Financial Management);

2. Consider a marketing campaign for launching a new service (Planning and Marketing);

3. Consider another malpractice carrier (Risk Management);

4. Assess the progress made in the electronic medical record project (Information Management);

5. Explore a new patient flow method (Clinical Operations);

6. Nominate a new board member (Governance);

7. Hear the Ethics Committee's recommendation on a patient-confidentiality issue (Professional Responsibility); and

8. Evaluate pension plan changes (Human Resource Management).

These topics cover the broad spectrum of medical practice tasks and situations in the eight Technical/Professional Knowledge and Skills performance domains, and require the medical practice executive to understand and apply each of them.

■ Summary

The practice executive requires proficiency and competency in the five general competencies of professionalism, leadership, communications, organizational and analytical skills, and technical/professional knowledge. The knowledge and skills needed in the Business and Clinical Operations domain are critical for the success of both the practice executive and the medical practice. By mastering this domain, the practice executive will be able to apply his or her talents to effectively lead the organization toward success.

Current Business and Clinical Operations Issues

WHEN LOOKING at the Business and Clinical Operations domain from a broad perspective, it is clear that this domain is in a state of change. It is apparent that the domain is in a state of evolution as it attempts to maintain balance while also changing to meet the demands and expectations of the individual stakeholders as well as society as a whole. The practice administrator should take the time to identify and understand the specific pressures of operations as well as those issues that are core within other domains but also affect this domain.

Numerous internal and external pressures affect the operational side of practice management. These pressures include, but are not limited to:

1. Regulatory changes at the federal, state, and local levels;

2. Third-party payer demands and expectations;

3. Patient demands and expectations;

4. Staff expectations;

5. Physician expectations; and

6. Community expectations.

Other key issues that affect the operational areas are well-represented in other domains. These issues include:

1. The effect of the Health Insurance Portability and Accountability Act of 1996 (HIPAA) regulation;

2. The ability to recruit and retain qualified staff; and

3. The need to control costs in a variety of areas, including staffing, supplies, regulatory demands, third-party contracting, and information management.

Knowledge
Needs

TO PROPERLY AND EFFECTIVELY RESPOND to the ongoing internal and external forces on both the practice and business of medicine, the practice executive should be well grounded in the fundamentals of day-to-day operations and the methodologies needed to maintain and improve the processes that affect organizations during these ever-evolving times. Expertise in these fundamental business and clinical skills is the ultimate goal. Several of the key skills include the ability to use project management techniques to measure and improve practice operations; the development and implementation of survey techniques to identify expectations and perceived shortcomings among various user groups; and the identification of organizational needs while evaluating, designing, and implementing changes to meet those needs. Finally, the medical practice executive needs to know how the various parts of the operation fit together and how they complement and support each other.

Business and Clinical Operations includes 10 distinct tasks, as identified in this volume. Each task is interconnected with the others through several strong identifiable threads, namely:

1. Analyzing how an organization accomplishes its tasks with an eye toward change;

2. Bringing all stakeholders into the process to ensure that everyone's needs are met in an effective and efficient manner without endangering others' needs;

3. Maintaining attention to detail – many tasks allow viewing the situation as a "big picture," but these tasks also require the administrator to ensure that all of the dots and dashes are in the right place;

4. Communicating the changes and improvements that are implemented to provide quality care and meet patient needs in a cost-effective manner.

Overview of Business and Clinical Operations Tasks

THE BASIC SKILLS of the Business and Clinical Operations domain are delineated within the 10 tasks outlined here. By exploring each specific task, it is possible to understand how it fits within the framework of the domain. Medical practice executives should develop and use their knowledge and skills to ensure that the following tasks related to business and clinical operations are carried out.

■ TASK 1: Facilitate business operations planning

This task emphasizes the difference between operational and strategic planning and how these key business functions must be incorporated into the organization's mission, vision, and values.

■ TASK 2: Conduct staffing analysis and scheduling

This task develops an understanding of the various issues within the realm of medical practice staffing, including (1) the proper number of staff and physicians with the correct mix of skills; (2) effective standardization of human resource policies that address employee concerns while clearly identifying and stating the needs and expectations of the organization; and (3) clear and concise procedures to address safety matters for patients and staff.

■ TASK 3: Develop ancillary clinical support services

This task presents opportunities to increase revenue streams by, for example, adding lab, X-ray, pharmacy, and rehabilitation to a practice's service menu. In addition, it addresses certification and licensing regulations, clinical quality-of-care standards, and various methods to evaluate the feasibility as well as the return on these investments.

■ TASK 4: Establish purchasing procurement and inventory control systems

Supplies and equipment are the tools that physicians and staff need to function and properly provide the services patients expect. This task presents information on purchasing standards, automated systems, inventory control, equipment purchase vs. lease, and ways to address the quality and safety of supplies.

■ TASK 5: Develop and implement facilities planning and maintenance programs

This task addresses facility design as it relates to physician/staff workflow, patient safety, and federal and state compliance. In addition, it touches on the multiple facets of facility management, including fire drills and evacuation, housekeeping standards, utility (heating, air conditioning, and ventilation) requirements, and the policies and procedures of the Occupational Safety and Health Administration (OSHA) and the Americans with Disabilities Act of 1990 (ADA).

■ TASK 6: Establish patient flow processes

Patient flow is one of the most important success predictors in any medical practice. This task will help the medical practice executive to evaluate and manage the practice's daily flow, including emergencies, queuing, cancellations, no-shows, and barriers. It addresses the key patient flow issues regarding business requirements, such as coding and financial screenings, as well as clinical requirements, such as encounter management, physician maximization, treatment plans, informed consent, referral processes, patient access, and confidentiality.

■ TASK 7: Develop and implement patient-communication systems

Communication systems are imperative to any business's success, and medical practices are no exception. Patients, staff, and physicians should be encouraged to embrace technology that can help the practice improve its performance. Communication systems, call centers, Internet-based technologies, patient-education programs, and technical know-how are just a partial list of what this task covers.

■ TASK 8: Develop clinical pathway structure and function

Clinical pathways, continuous quality improvement, and clinical outcomes data models and analysis are covered in this task. Topics covered include multidisciplinary teams; the impact of redundancy; external agencies and payers; quality assurance programs; chart reviews; and evaluating physician, payer, and patient-satisfaction data.

■ TASK 9: **Create monitoring systems for licensure, credentialing, and recertification**

Within any accreditation process, an organization can expect that the following evaluations will be reviewed: governing bylaws, safety and health procedures, facility design and safety, chart documentation, human resources, quality assurance reviews, and physician and staff credentialing. This task addresses these topics as well as the development, implementation, and adherence to documented policies and procedures that delineate and govern the day-to-day operations of the practice.

■ TASK 10: **Develop and implement process improvement programs for clinic operations**

Growth, change, and evolution constitute every successful practice's goals. One primary reason to develop and implement process improvement programs is to constantly test the organization's own core processes and create ways to improve operations, as addressed in this task.

TASK 1 # Facilitate Business Operations Planning

"PLANNING IS A PROCESS by which management visualizes the future and develops specific courses of action to achieve organizational goals."[1] To set a proper foundation for the business operations planning process, it is important to first set a strategic framework plan and clearly articulate the organization's mission, vision, and values.

Strategic planning seeks to formulate those organizational goals and plans that normally take five to ten years to accomplish. Strategic planning also requires the administrator to take a long-term view of the organizational environment and base plans on the present business environment, and it demands that the planning be constantly updated to evolve and respond to the ever-changing external and internal dynamics. The *strategic plan* is therefore a dynamic document that must be constantly updated.

The *mission statement* defines the unique and distinctive purpose of the organization. It should be succinct and to the point without promising something that the organization cannot provide or prove, such as a statement that the organization provides the "highest" level of care in the area. In summary, the mission statement should state who the organization is and what it is about.

To determine where the organization needs to grow or change in the future, it is helpful to create a *vision statement*. Whereas the mission statement conveys what the

17

organization is today, the vision statement communicates what the organization wants to be in the future. Although this statement is normally the "dream" of the organization, it should have a basis in reality or it will become irrelevant to both the staff within the organization and anyone else desirous of learning about the goals of the organization.

The last document used to create the planning framework is the *values statement.* The values statement defines the culture of the organization and, by doing so, clearly states the ethics and principles that guide the organization and all of its members.[2]

Operational, or tactical, planning addresses the more immediate, short-term needs of an organization and supports or complements the strategic plan. Operational planning includes such issues as planning for staff vacation coverage or developing a budget for the next year. Because operational plans have a much shorter life span, they are not as affected as strategic plans by changes in external and internal dynamics. The importance of operational planning is to create a foundation that can be used by departments and other components of the organization to develop their own plans and budgets. The development of these operational plans should take into account the mission and vision of the organization as well as the resources that are available to meet the plans and goals of the organization. This operational or tactical plan, in addressing short-term or relatively immediate issues, should include several components, such as:

1. Identifying and defining the problem or issue to be addressed;

2. Identifying the goal that will define the completion of this plan as a success;

3. Identifying the resources (e.g., personnel, equipment, supplies, space, and funding) needed to complete the plan;

4. Determining the time line for competing the plan; and

5. Identifying the potential interactions with other stakeholders and affected parties.

For planning to work, the strategies and tactics to be employed must be consistent with the culture of the organization. The culture of the organization sets the tone for how the organization will project itself to the outside world as well as how it will act internally from an operational perspective and through interactions among the various staff and providers. This culture both emanates from and is affected by the goals, perspectives, background, and ethics of the leadership in addition to the impact of the demographics and expectations of the surrounding community in which the practice is located. Developing the culture necessary for supportive buy-in requires proactive initiatives by the physician as well as the administrative leadership. The development of the values statement that was previously discussed is helpful in identifying the internal culture of the organization. The organization's culture should also acknowledge and be responsive to any individual cultural barriers or differences that may exist among the various stakeholders of the organization.

Whenever change is being contemplated within an organization, there often is concern. Some of this concern emanates from the physicians, who are not always able to understand the difference between the practice of medicine and the business of health care. Physicians become proficient in the practice of medicine during residencies and fellowships, but practice managers should help physicians understand and come to grips with the requirements, and often conflicting demands, of the business of health care. For example, an orthopedic physician may want to add radiology services to the practice without first conducting feasibility plans or formally assessing the opportunity by looking at the community's ability to support the service. It is the manager's responsibility to explain and show physicians why the operations and strategic plans including (or not including) such opportunities are important and appropriate for the practice's future.

Through the use of management-led working committees, supervisory councils, and staff meetings, physicians and staff will become more understanding of, and comfortable with, the structure of the operations plan. Through such education, physicians and staff can become integral parts of the planning process, thereby helping to evolve and grow a corporate culture that embraces both planning and change.

TASK 2 **Conduct Staffing Analysis and Scheduling**

PHYSICIANS ARE THE KEY PROVIDERS and leaders within a medical practice, but they cannot accomplish all of the required tasks of the practice by themselves. The skills and the time required for meeting all of the daily tasks and obligations of the organization demand employment of a variety of personnel. This group of personnel includes clinical staff, such as medical assistants, nurses, and technicians, as well as clerical/administrative staff, which may include medical billers, receptionists, bookkeepers, and file clerks. Key issues within the realm of staffing include (1) the proper number of staff with the correct mix of skills, (2) effective standardized human resource policies that address employee concerns while clearly identifying and stating the needs and expectations of the organization, and (3) clear and concise procedures to address the safety concerns that are prevalent within a medical practice.

Therefore, one of the most critical aspects of a practice is staffing. In the majority of practices, staffing makes up the most significant percentage of overhead expense. According to the MGMA *Cost Survey for Multispecialty Practices: 2005 Report Based on 2004 Data*, the median staff cost for a multispecialty practice not owned by a hospital, regardless of size, is 29.04 percent of total medical revenue, representing about 50 percent of total operating cost. The staff is therefore not only the largest expense of the organization, it is also one the most important assets of the organization. Normally, a patient's first contact with the practice is an employee, either at the reception desk or via telephone. This interaction sets the stage for everything to follow. An employee who feels appreciated and supported in his or her working environment is more likely to present the face and voice of the organization in a positive and inviting manner. All aspects of staffing should therefore be continually reviewed and analyzed to ensure that the organization is utilizing this critical asset in the most efficient and effective manner possible.

The medical practice executive should address multiple issues when analyzing staffing within the organization. Normally, the first question that comes to mind is "Do we have enough staff?" Effective staffing analysis, however, requires an in-depth review of numerous other factors, including the mix of full-time and part-time staff, compensation and benefits, utilization of overtime, documentation and application of personnel policies, turnover rates, and the needs of the organization. In addition, staffing demands may be affected by clinical needs and safety concerns that are normally specialty-specific. An example of staffing differences that are specialty-driven is demonstrated in comparing an orthopedic practice with an oncology practice. The clinical needs of an orthopedic practice would include the hiring of primarily medical assistants, cast technicians, and radiology technologists, as the clinical staff normally provides supportive services for the physician and radiological examinations. An oncology practice, which would normally be providing a large amount of intravenous chemotherapy services, would rely very heavily on registered nurses, based upon their expertise and their legally defined skill sets, to provide this level of service.

The numbers and type of staff required by a specific organization can also vary significantly based upon many factors, including centralized vs. decentralized functions (e.g., scheduling and billing); the physicians' office setting and specialty (hospital-based vs. clinic-based); the physical structure of the organization (single-office vs. multiple sites); and the utilization of ancillary services (e.g., physical therapy, clinical laboratory, pulmonary testing, and phototherapy). In addition, the demands on staffing may also be greatly affected by the service expectations of both the physicians of the organization as well as the community that is served by the practice. For example, a plastic surgery practice that provides upscale cosmetic surgery services would be expected to have available a significantly higher staffing ratio to meet the desires of patients who are requesting elective services that are not normally covered by insurance but are paid solely "out of pocket."

In evaluating the staffing of an organization, it is helpful for the medical practice executive to apply various appropriate, quantifiable benchmarks. The term "benchmark" is defined as a standard of measurement or evaluation, such as an average, median, or percentile. The data needed to compare a specific organization with external benchmarks is available from various sources, which can be local, regional, or national. Some examples of operational measurements that are easily benchmarked within a practice include days in accounts receivables, number of personnel by type per full-time equivalent (FTE) physician, overhead rate, collection ratio, and employee salary and benefit packages.

Whereas staffing benchmarks are normally based upon national or regional data, salary and benefit surveys are more effective when based on state or local information. Good sources for national benchmarks can be found within MGMA or various specialty societies, and local salary and benefits information can best be found through state and local chapters of MGMA as well as local chambers of commerce. Because benchmarks are based upon data from many practices, variations from a particular practice's information will occur. Variations are not necessarily causes for alarm, but they are catalysts to identify those areas that require review and analysis.

Another factor that has a significant effect on the demands and needs of the staffing pattern within an organization is the design and process for scheduling patients who are cared for by the organization. The scheduling system is critical to the successful operation of the practice because it allows patients access to the practice and contributes to the most efficient use of provider time and resources.[3] The scheduling system is normally the patient's first interaction with the practice, and it sets the tone for future communication between the patient and the practice. The ease of obtaining an appointment with a provider within the practice assists in setting the patient's level of expectation for service and responsiveness. The scheduling system also sets the basis for the flow of patients within the organization.

Various organizations use different types of scheduling formats, based in part upon the culture of the organization, the physician specialties, and the patient population. Patient flow and its effect on the organization is discussed in more detail in Task 6, "Establish Patient Flow Processes," but is summarized briefly here. The more common scheduling methodologies include block time, modified wave, and individual scheduling. In block time scheduling, a group of patients are told to arrive at the same time (e.g., five patients on each hour). In a modified wave schedule, three patients might arrive on the hour, another patient twenty minutes later, and a fifth patient twenty minutes after that. Individual scheduling is accomplished just as the name implies, with each patient given a specific time in the schedule. Each of these methodologies has its own strengths and weaknesses and should be applied only after analyzing the needs of the organization and the expectations of the patients and the providers.

The final issue is that of safety, which has both direct and indirect effects on the organization. When addressing safety, an organization should provide sufficient time and resources to ensure that staff are properly trained in all aspects of safety, including infection control, environmental hazards (e.g., fire and electrical), and medication errors. These issues also have a direct effect on patients and the need to educate them on various issues of safety, including pharmaceutical management and infection control. In addition, many of these items have an indirect affect on the bottom line through issues of risk management, which encompasses the costs associated with staff and patient injuries, as well as general liability of the organization if proper care is not taken to secure, control, and properly manage the supplies/equipment and the by-products of their use.

For further discussion and examples on staffing, readers should refer to volume 5 of the *Medical Practice Management Body of Knowledge Review: Human Resource Management*.

Develop Ancillary Clinical Support Services

THE TERM "ANCILLARY SERVICES" has different meanings when defined by physicians of different specialties. The general definition of ancillary services refers to those services that are supplementary to the direct services provided by the physician. In addition, these services provide another source of revenue for the organization. As examples, an orthopedic practice's ancillary services may include radiology, magnetic resonance imaging, bone densitometry, and physical and occupational therapy. A gastroenterology practice may include infusions and virtual endoscopy, whereas an internal medicine practice may look to radiology, electrocardiogram, pulmonary function testing, clinical laboratory, Holter monitors, and stress testing. A multispecialty practice would avail itself of many different ancillary services, of which a majority may be utilized by more than one specialty.

Just as there are many different types of ancillary services, there are also several reasons for a practice to provide such services. There is the issue of patients desiring "one-stop shopping," with the ability to receive a significant amount of the services ordered by the physician at a single location, supported by the knowledge that the physician will be providing oversight to ensure that the test or service is provided properly. Within the organization, increased pressures by insurance carriers to reduce the reimbursement rates that are being paid to practices have forced practices to identify new sources of revenue that can be provided by ancillary staff and not add significant time demands on physicians' already busy schedules. As reported in *MGMA Connexion*[4] and as shown in Exhibit 1, the addition of ancillary services can have a significant effect on both the profitability of a practice and the income of a physician.

Prior to adding an ancillary service, the practice should take a diligent approach to analyzing the positive and negative ramifications of adding a specific ancillary service. The various aspects of this analysis and goal setting make up the operational planning process. A cost/benefit analysis should be done that reviews the projected demand for the service vs. the cost of providing the service and the anticipated revenue. An ancillary service that is projected to lose revenue should be avoided. In some situations, an organization will add an ancillary service that is projected to break even because of the noneconomic benefits of providing that service. These noneconomic benefits may include responding to issues of nonavailability of the service within the community or the level of quality of the service currently available within the community but outside of the practice. The analysis to determine the noneconomic benefits of a new service rests heavily on identifying and reviewing the clinical reasons for adding the service under discussion.

As part of the analysis for adding ancillary services, consideration should be given to the different methodologies for providing the service in question. Practices can develop, purchase, and provide a service themselves and retain all revenues that are derived from it. When the practice retains all of the revenues derived from an ancillary service, it also assumes all of the risks and expenses incurred in providing, managing, and maintaining that ancillary service. Other options to be explored for providing the desired ancillary service include outsourcing the service to another entity, purchasing the service from an outside vendor, subcontracting the service, and, finally, joint venturing with another entity. In each of these other scenarios, the practice shares, in varying degrees, the financial risks and incentives of each ancillary service.

Regardless of the methodology used to provide the service, the practice should ensure that the methodology and structure chosen

EXHIBIT 1.

How ancillary services affect performance and profitability

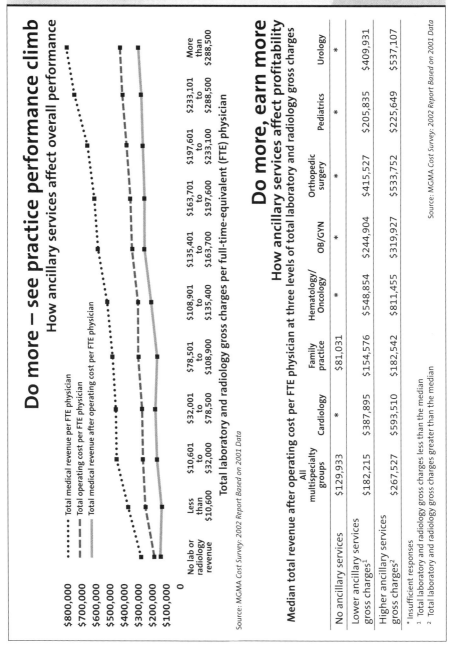

Do more – see practice performance climb
How ancillary services affect overall performance

- •••••••• Total medical revenue per FTE physician
- – – – – Total operating cost per FTE physician
- ———— Total medical revenue after operating cost per FTE physician

Total laboratory and radiology gross charges per full-time-equivalent (FTE) physician

$800,000
$700,000
$600,000
$500,000
$400,000
$300,000
$200,000
$100,000
0

| | No lab or radiology revenue | Less than $10,600 | $10,601 to $32,000 | $32,001 to $78,500 | $78,501 to $108,900 | $108,901 to $135,400 | $135,401 to $163,700 | $163,701 to $197,600 | $197,601 to $233,100 | $233,101 to $288,500 | More than $288,500 |

Source: MGMA Cost Survey: 2002 Report Based on 2001 Data

Do more, earn more
How ancillary services affect profitability

Median total revenue after operating cost per FTE physician at three levels of total laboratory and radiology gross charges

	All multispecialty groups	Cardiology	Family practice	Hematology/ Oncology	OB/GYN	Orthopedic surgery	Pediatrics	Urology
No ancillary services	$129,933	*	$81,031	*	*	*	*	*
Lower ancillary services gross charges[1]	$182,215	$387,895	$154,576	$548,854	$244,904	$415,527	$205,835	$409,931
Higher ancillary services gross charges[2]	$267,527	$593,510	$182,542	$811,455	$319,927	$533,752	$225,649	$537,107

* Insufficient responses
[1] Total laboratory and radiology gross charges less than the median
[2] Total laboratory and radiology gross charges greater than the median

Source: MGMA Cost Survey: 2002 Report Based on 2001 Data

are in compliance with the federal, state, and local regulatory guidelines that may apply to and affect the provision of the designated ancillary service. In some cases, it is also necessary that the organization obtain specific licensure and/or certifications to provide and bill for the clinical ancillary services. For example, when adding clinical laboratory services to a practice, it is necessary that all government regulations are met, and that the entity providing the clinical laboratory services is in full compliance with the federal Clinical Laboratory Improvement Act (CLIA), with local and state licensing requirements, and with third-party payer credentialing. Depending on the structure of the entity providing the service, it may be necessary to ensure compliance with both Stark I and Stark II. Based upon adherence to both Stark I and Stark II guidelines, some of the methodologies chosen may no longer be viable alternatives, as they may no longer comply with some of the self-referral regulations as promulgated by the Stark guidelines. A simple example would be the failure to meet the requirements of in-office ancillary testing while attempting to joint venture with another entity for such services. Finally, contracting demands are crucial to the success of adding an ancillary service.

In addition to external regulatory issues, the practice should ensure that the clinical ancillary services that are provided meet defined quality standards. Quality standards are evaluated through the use of various outcomes measurements. This includes proficiency testing, whereby blind samples are provided by external organizations and the results are compared with the previously determined results from the external agency. Outcomes measurements are extremely difficult to quantify and normally cannot be properly done using a single standard or evaluation point. The measuring and evaluation of outcomes can result from individual actions, such as chart reviews; auditing of various clinical activities (e.g., patient satisfaction surveys, abnormal test results, and incident reports); and auditing of specific diagnoses or procedures to ensure that proper protocols and procedures are followed.

To effectively manage and monitor the provision of these services, it is important that services are properly integrated into the operations of the practice's infrastructure. This is best done through the implementation of a robust information management system that ties together all of the business and clinical aspects of the practice. No single system is capable of providing for all of the information needs of a practice, so unique individual components and programs should be identified that are compatible and can be effectively interfaced to provide a workable system that meets the needs of the practice. These needs vary, of course, based upon the specialties being served. In all cases, these information systems must be secure from outside influences to ensure patient confidentiality and compliance with HIPAA regulations and guidelines.

These services will need to be documented in the patient's medical record and properly accounted for within the practice management system for billing and collection purposes. In cases of consumable items, inventory systems should be initiated with appropriate reorder points set, and fixed assets need to be maintained in proper working order. Periodic operational and financial evaluations should also be completed to ensure that the ancillary service being provided is meeting the clinical goals as well as the strategic and operational plan of the organization while providing the projected profit margins for the organization.

TASK 4 # Establish Purchasing Procurement and Inventory Control Systems

SUPPLIES AND EQUIPMENT are the tools that physicians and staff need to function and provide the services that are expected of them. Supplies and equipment include waiting-room chairs and copy paper; consumables, such as scanners, vaccines, and radiology systems; and computers and sophisticated, expensive medical equipment.

These purchases are normally divided into three basic groups: fixed assets, nonbillable supplies, and billable supplies. Fixed assets comprise equipment and instruments that can be used on multiple occasions. They appear on the balance sheet of the practice as an asset and are expensed through the application of depreciation. Nonbillable supplies are those consumables that are used as part of normal everyday operations. The costs of these items cannot be billed to the patient, but they are sometimes billed to specific departments within a practice when detailed cost accounting is desired. Examples of these consumables are pens, paper, alcohol swabs, and syringes.

The last major grouping comprises billable supplies. These are consumable items for which the cost can be passed on to either the patient and/or the third-party payer. The types of supplies included in this category vary based upon the specialty of the physician and the rules and regulations that may exist for the state in which the practice is located. Some examples of these billable supplies and the type of practice most likely to stock them are skin care products in dermatology, braces and splints in orthopedics, vaccines in pediatrics and internal medicine, and nutritional supplements in obstetrics. In some cases, the costs of these consumables are not covered by the third-party payer and become the responsibility of the patient. An example of this would be a waterproof casting material instead of standard plaster if a parent whose child has broken an arm or leg wishes the physician to use such an option. The additional cost of this material is normally not covered by the third-party payer, and the patient or guarantor is responsible for the additional cost.

Unless properly controlled, the purchase, storage, and usage of both billable and nonbillable supplies can become a significant drain on the financial status of the practice. Therefore, guidelines and operating procedures for the ordering, use, and monitoring of supplies should be initiated and maintained. Some examples of these guidelines and procedures are:

- Determination of a schedule for ordering specific groupings of supplies (e.g., clinical, office, pharmaceutical);

- Use of standardized order forms that spell out the specific items that may be ordered;

- Determination of minimum and maximum reorder points to ensure that the organization neither runs out of critical supplies nor stockpiles supplies in quantities that would be categorized as wasteful (these reorder points should be set so that inventory turns over or is completely replaced eight to ten times per year); and

- Periodic checking of the purchase of billable supplies against the amounts that are actually billed to patients. The amounts billed to patients when added to the inventory on hand should equal the amount purchased by the practice. If the amount purchased is higher than the total of the amount billed plus inventory, then the reasons for the inventory shrinkage should be investigated and corrected.

The larger the organization, the greater the importance of developing and implementing standards for the various consumable products to ensure that the practice does not begin to maintain stocks of multiple brands of the same product based upon the desires of individual members of the organization. By standardizing the consumable products purchased and maintaining specific minimum and maximum reorder points, a practice can maximize savings and reduce costs. Other steps that can be taken to reduce the expenses incurred for consumables include periodically checking prices among various suppliers to ensure the best price and negotiating longer-term contracts whereby the practice is committing to purchase specified products from a supplier for fixed prices.

When purchasing equipment, other issues should be addressed to assure that the practice receives the greatest value for the dollar expended. Whether for meeting clinical or administrative demands, the purchaser needs to evaluate the different models and types of equipment available on the market. In addition to evaluating whether the equipment will meet the operational needs of the organization, the costs of the equipment, including acquisition costs (whether purchase or lease), cost of supplies needed to maintain the equipment, maintenance contracts, and any construction renovations needed to maintain and operate the equipment should be assessed. Once the final decision is made on the specific make and model of equipment to be purchased, it is the responsibility of the designated administrative officer to not only negotiate the best offer for the equipment but to periodically evaluate the equipment to ensure that it continues to meet the organization's needs in an efficient and cost-effective manner.

In addition, the purchaser should consider that the utilization of these supplies will result in the creation of various waste products that must be disposed of in a proper and timely manner. Arrangements should be made to properly dispose of biohazardous waste products, including syringes, sharps (e.g., needles and scalpels), and any products that have been contaminated with bodily fluids and blood. Failure to properly dispose of these items can result in an exposure risk to other patients and staff. Normally, this type of disposal is handled through contracts with licensed companies.

A second significant waste product issue involves the disposal of documentation that may contain a patient's name and other private information. These waste documents may include daily appointment schedules and duplicate telephone messages. To ensure compliance with HIPAA guidelines, all of these documents should be properly shredded, which involves either obtaining the equipment necessary to internally shred the documents in question or contracting with an independent, bonded shredding company to perform this task and provide receptacles to secure the documents until they are properly destroyed.

A final category of supplies, which touches upon all of the previous areas of discussion and has several additional issues, are pharmaceuticals. Within a practice, this category may have several distinct subgroupings, based upon the practice's specialty. These subgroupings may include vaccines, injectible medications (e.g., Solu-Medrol, Depo-Medrol, vitamin B-12), narcotics, and samples of prescription medications. With the exception of samples, all of these items would be considered billable consumable supplies.

The maintenance of pharmaceutical supplies within a practice is subject to various federal, state, and local regulations and laws. Narcotics and other controlled substances must be kept in secured locations (e.g., double-locked safes or metal boxes) that are not accessible to unauthorized staff or others. In addition, logs must be kept of the utilization of these drugs, and periodic confirmatory inventories must be accomplished. The logs for each pharmaceutical should document the final disposition of all narcotics and controlled substances purchased or received by the practice. All of these documents must be available to designated government investigators charged with the responsibility to ensure compliance with regulatory safeguards.

The practice needs to ensure that all other pharmaceuticals are appropriately secured and dispensed in a clinically correct and safe manner. Because many pharmaceuticals and vaccines have significant costs and short shelf lives, the practice should implement and maintain strong inventory systems, including rotation of stock to ensure that inventory does not reach its expiration date, tracking of utilization to ensure that all usage has been properly billed, and proper disposal of out-of-date items. Many out-of-date pharmaceuticals can be returned to the manufacturer or supplier for credit toward new inventory. Additionally, this inventory should be kept in centralized locked cabinets to ensure that they will be properly maintained and distributed.

The use of pharmaceutical samples within practices has become a significant issue of control, storage, and maintenance. The practice may be inundated with pharmaceutical sales representatives whose function is to provide information on why their particular pharmaceutical is the best as well as to provide the practice with samples for patient use. The practice needs to set inventory controls in place when accepting these samples, or the practice may find itself with significant excess quantities of a specific drug. Once the practice has accepted these samples for distribution to patients, it has also accepted responsibility for the proper storage, control, and the ultimate disposal of these samples. The same inventory problems and issues that are addressed with pharmaceuticals that are purchased by the practice also should apply to these pharmaceutical samples. Most practices secure the samples in cabinets or closets that are locked when the practice is closed. Because of the volume involved, a major issue for a practice is the disposal of samples that have passed their expiration date. These samples cannot be returned to the manufacturer, and the responsibility falls upon the practice to properly dispose of them. This disposal process can become extremely time-consuming and expensive for the practice.

All of these items directly affect the bottom line of the organization. As such, it is important for the medical practice executive to monitor these costs and track them within the appropriate department or cost center.

Develop and Implement Facilities Planning and Maintenance Programs

THE DESIGN, construction, maintenance, and appearance of a practice's offices are critical to the efficiency of the practice. As with any business or place of public accommodation, the outward appearance of a facility sets a foundation for the client/patient's expectation of the level and quality of service that will be provided. Facilities that are dark with threadbare carpeting and dingy walls will be perceived by clients as providing second-rate service; facilities that are well lit, clean, and neat will be perceived as providing a much higher level of service.

The design or layout of a facility, although normally transparent to the patient, will have far-reaching effects on the efficiency of the physicians and staff. Clinical areas that are designed to allow easy access to the supplies and support services that may be required during the course of the day will enable physicians and staff to be more productive and effective. Failure to be attentive to proper office design may result in a variety of problems, including physicians and staff becoming overtired because of excessive walking and the duplication of expensive supply inventories within examination rooms in an effort to reduce these walking demands.

When the opportunity exists to either design a new facilities plan, or significantly renovate an existing space, it is best to utilize the expertise of an architect who is well versed and experienced in the design and construction of medical office space. In designing or renovating facilities, applicable building codes and regulations have to be integrated. These issues, which span local, state, and federal agencies, create a range of structural requirements that require compliance to ensure a safe environment. In most instances, local building codes will provide the requirements for construction issues, including wiring and plumbing standards; width of corridors; and heating, ventilation, and air conditioning (HVAC) minimums. Sufficient insulation between rooms and noise-dampening materials should also be used in construction to help ensure patient privacy.

Federal guidelines that require compliance are primarily represented by the regulations of the Americans with Disabilities Act of 1990 (ADA) and the Occupational Safety and Health Administration (OSHA). The primary goal of the ADA, as it applies to facilities, is to ensure that individuals with disabilities have safe and easy access to and can maneuver within a place of public accommodation. To comply within the parameters of the ADA, a practice needs to address physical design features such as ensuring that doors are wide enough to allow for the passage of a wheelchair, having restroom facilities available that can be easily used by the disabled, and providing adequate designated handicapped parking. In cases where the physical space is not owned by the practice, meeting these expectations will be the responsibility of the building management.

The safety of staff, patients, and visitors is addressed through adherence to the regulations set forth by OSHA. These safety issues include the proper maintenance, use, and storage of equipment, or addressing any hazardous situation, such as loose extension cords and boxes that are stacked too high. Other safety issues concern access to proper fire prevention equipment and the installation of security alarms and/or cameras, where appropriate. In addition to setting forth guidelines and regulations to assure the safety of patients, visitors, and staff, OSHA regulations require the organization to maintain logs and information on all accidents and injuries that occur on the premises. Through these reports, issues affecting the safety and well-being of everyone are maintained.

When designing or renovating a facility, attentiveness to small details that enable a facility to be both efficient and attractive are important. Patients and visitors coming to the facility require appropriate signage to assist them in reaching the correct office or location within the practice. Adequate signage also is important to assist new employees in becoming familiar with the office and building layout. Appropriate color schemes for walls, flooring, and furniture are helpful in maintaining a relaxing and inviting environment for patients who might otherwise be stressful and anxious.

In addition to the design of the clinical areas, attention should be paid to the business areas of the practice, which patients never see, including billing, scheduling, medical records, accounting, human resources, and storage. Failure to design these areas properly and to provide for sufficient storage space will have a direct negative impact on the ability of the support staff to adequately complete their job assignments.

No matter how well a facility is designed and decorated, though, without proper preventive maintenance, the significant investment that is made in creating the facility will soon lose its value. Preventive maintenance includes such day-to-day issues as trash removal, vacuuming, dusting, and mopping. In addition, other maintenance items need to be scheduled on a regular basis, including window washing, touch-up painting, replacement of dim or burned-out bulbs, and minor cosmetic repairs of furniture and equipment. Patients are very quick to identify housekeeping issues and equate them to the quality of the medical services provided. Although patients may not comment when facilities are clean and well maintained, they do notice (and comment) when their expectations are not met, and they apply their observations to determining the professionalism and quality of the physicians of the practice.

The concept of facility design and maintenance goes beyond the confines of the four walls of the practice's office; attention should also be paid to ensuring that adequate, safe parking is available and that the grounds surrounding the building are properly maintained and landscaped. The building should appear inviting, without dark corridors or foreboding entranceways. Patients have choices of where to obtain their medical services, and it is incumbent upon the practice to provide a safe and welcoming environment.

TASK 6 **Establish Patient Flow Processes**

FOR A PRACTICE TO BE EFFICIENT and allow the physician and staff to focus on patient care, attention should be paid to how work flows within the organization. This workflow, from a patient's perspective, includes the four primary steps of (1) making an appointment, (2) entering the office, (3) receiving treatment from the physician, and, finally, (4) leaving the office as a satisfied recipient of high-quality medical care.

In addition to patient-centered workflow are other distinctly separate workflows for business and clinical processes that do not directly affect, nor are they seen by, the patient. Analysis of patient flow should be undertaken, including the posting of charges and payments, filing of medical records, and processing of medical record copy requests. Examples of this type of analysis as applied to the first stage of the patient-centered and business workflows are shown in Exhibits 2a and 2b.[5] Although patients do not see the behind-the-scenes workflows, they are affected by any breakdowns that occur within these flows. A significant portion of patient satisfaction with the practice is determined by the efficiency, accuracy, and effectiveness of the steps that are accomplished behind the scenes.

EXHIBIT 2a.
Typical patient flow process at check-in

Current check-in process

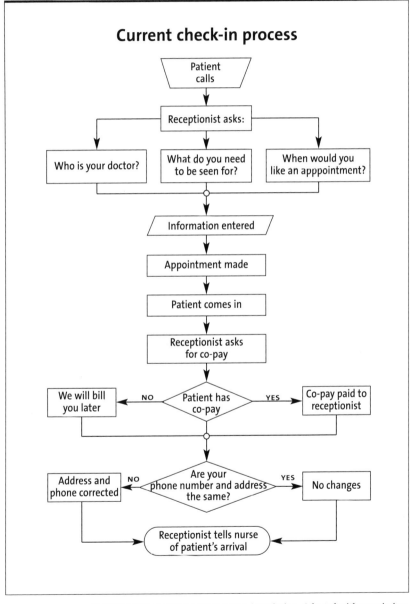

Efficient patient flow process at check-in

New check-in process

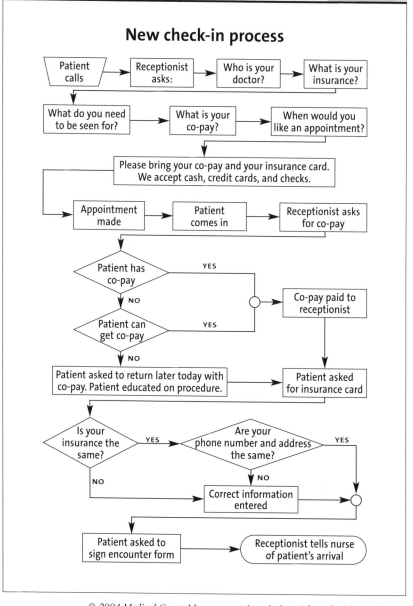

The framework or initial anticipated flow for patient activity is determined by the day's schedule of appointments. "Good scheduling demands good planning, good data, good information systems, and, above all, good staff; that is, workers who are trained, committed, and empowered to provide top-notch customer service."[6] To properly develop an appointment schedule that allows the provider to be efficient, and to anticipate staffing needs, the development of patient demand projections based on several factors, including patient demand variations, should be conducted based on the day of the week and time of day; age of patients, which can affect the amount of time needed for the provider/patient interaction; and the specialty and personality of the physician, which can also affect the amount of time needed for the provider/patient interaction.

Other factors that can affect a daily schedule, but cannot be as easily projected, include emergencies; calls from hospitals, nursing homes, and other physicians; and last-minute cancellations and no-shows. Some of these issues can be anticipated, and schedule modifications and office procedures can be implemented in an effort to reduce their negative effects. A variety of different scheduling methodologies can be used to alleviate some of these variations. The scheduling methodology that would alleviate these concerns to the greatest degree would be a block schedule, as discussed previously, by which several patients are told to come in at the same time (e.g., on the hour) and are seen based upon their time of arrival. This method does reduce the issues of gaps and providers waiting for delayed and no-show patients, but it also increases patient waiting time.[7] To reduce the risk of no-shows, staff can be assigned or computer systems implemented to call patients to remind them of their appointments, appointment slots can be held open to allow for last-minute add-ons, and the judicious use of double booking can be implemented to compensate for last-minute cancellations and no-shows that do occur.

Issues that may upset or aggravate patients during the patient workflow cycle may include extensive delays in the waiting room, not being advised to bring specific documents with them to the appointment with the physician, extended waiting times in the examination room, and the inability to get timely follow-up appointments when leaving the offices of the practice. Many of these outcomes can be avoided by simple patient communication. When confirming appointments, practices should remind patients of the documents and forms that they should bring to their appointments. Many of these forms are unique to specific insurance carriers (e.g., Medicare, Medicaid, employer plans, and commercial carriers), and plans and may include referrals and procedure precertifications. Communicating with the patient, explaining what is going on, and reassuring the patient can usually mitigate any annoyance or aggravation on the patient's part. Sufficient time should also be included within each visit to allow the physician to dictate notes and to respond to issues that became known during the visit with the patient.

The clinical flow within a practice is integral to assuring that patients receive effective and efficient care. Clinical flow begins long before the patient arrives in the practice's offices. Examination rooms need to be stocked, preferably in a standardized manner, with the supplies that may be required by the physician or staff. By standardizing both the items to be stored in each examination room and their locations within each examination room, staff will be able to reduce the amount of time needed to search for a specific everyday item. An alternative to maintaining stocks of supplies within each examination room is the use of small supply rooms or cabinets close to several examination rooms. Although potentially increasing the walking required of the clinical support staff, this method of maintaining supply stocks will reduce the overall amount of supplies that need to be maintained in inventory.

Medical records need to be retrieved and reviewed before the patient's arrival to ensure that all test results are available and that any required instruments or testing materials are available for the physician's use. Preplanning each visit and ensuring that the required information and supplies are available can reduce the amount of time needed for each visit, thereby enabling the physician to be more efficient in the use of his or her time.

Upon arrival, the patient begins the direct, on-site involvement by checking in at the practice's reception desk. At that time, the patient is identified and greeted by the reception staff. A new patient is normally asked to complete various intake documents providing the demographic and billing/insurance information that the practice needs to initiate a medical record and bill the appropriate source for payment. An established patient will normally be asked to confirm the information on file to ensure that no changes have taken place since the last office visit. The patient may then be asked to provide co-payment and any referral documents that may be appropriate. After completion of the required paperwork, a member of the clinical support staff normally escorts the patient to an examination room.

In addition to the direct hands-on care provided by both the physician and the clinical staff for the patient are several other areas within the clinical encounter that may require action by the physician or staff. These tasks, based upon the needs of the patient, may include:

1. Developing and documenting a treatment plan that addresses the patient's medical needs;

2. Providing needed educational support to the patient, which may include reviewing a videotape or providing printed material on the issues that concern the patient;

3. Ensuring that the patient has provided informed consent for procedures that are being scheduled;

4. Addressing HIV and other communicable-disease issues that may be of concern to the patient and others; and

5. Initiating any referrals or other carrier-required documents that may be needed by the patient to obtain the care indicated in the plan of treatment.

After providing the services that are required by the patient, the remainder of the clinical workflow for the staff consists of escorting the patient from the examination area and cleaning and preparing the examination room for the next patient. For the patient, the final step is checkout, where he or she will receive the required documents and forms, make any future appointments with the practice, and pay for any financial amounts that may be due and were not collected at time of check-in. For the physician, the final part of the clinical workflow process is made up of properly documenting the patient history, the clinical services provided, and the plan for future services. The last step for the physician – determining the procedure and diagnostic codes to be used to categorize this patient's visit – begins the second half of the business workflow process.

The business workflow identifies, collects, and processes all of the information required to properly and accurately bill for the services rendered by the practice. The business workflow begins when the patient calls to make the first appointment with the physician. At the time of making that first appointment, the practice should begin the process of obtaining the demographic information concerning the patient. This demographic information includes name, address, telephone number, guarantor, insurance information, and employer. At this time, the practice will normally confirm that the practice participates in the patient's insurance plan. The collection of demographic information continues when the patient arrives at the practice and provides a copy of an insurance card and, if appropriate, a referral from a primary care physician, and completes and signs the documents required by the practice. These documents normally include an intake registration form that details all of the patient's demographic information, a medical history, an authorization to assign the patient's insurance benefits to the practice, and a confirmation that the patient has been advised of the practice's HIPAA policies.

The procedure and diagnostic codes that the physician determines upon completion of the appointment will be used to categorize the services rendered. In many practices, this information is provided on a paper form that may variously be called a charge ticket, routing sheet, or trip ticket. This form will also indicate the additional billable services provided by either the physician or the support staff. These services may include immunizations or other injectable medications, X-rays, splints, or clinical laboratory services. In practices that use an electronic health record (EHR), the proper procedure codes may be generated directly from the physician's notes and posted to the patient's account within the practice management system.

It is this code determination that initiates the second phase of the business workflow. During this phase of the business workflow, the process of billing and collection takes place. The patient's insurance is reviewed and the required co-payment is collected, although in many offices this portion of the process is accomplished before the patient sees the physician. The determination of when the co-pay is collected is often a function of the physical layout of the office. The charge ticket is then reviewed for completeness, and the charges and the co-payment received are posted to the patient's account. Some offices post the charges in batches, whereas other offices post them as each patient leaves the office. There is no specific right or wrong way, as it is totally dependent on the workflow design within the specific office and the volume of visits and services. At the end of each day the posted batches of charges and payments received are closed out, meaning that all charge tickets and payments are accounted for and posted. The remaining business process consists of transmitting the charges to the appropriate third-party payers, applying the payments received from these payers to the appropriate patient account, posting any applicable contractual adjustments, and finally billing the patient or secondary insurance for any remaining balance. Interspersed within this process are the needs to respond to carrier requests for additional information, to appeal carrier denials of coverage or incorrect application of billing guidelines, and to respond to patient questions and requests for assistance in complying with the demands of the insurance carrier.

Throughout the process, and at all subsequent times, the practice must take all steps necessary to ensure patient confidentiality with respect to the medical treatment and status. All staff should be trained in the requirements of HIPAA regulations, and employee policies need to be specific in communicating the expectations of the practice that patient confidentiality is paramount within the organization.

TASK 7 **Develop and Implement Patient- Communication Systems**

THE NEEDS AND REQUIREMENTS of those who will be the users of the communication systems that are put into operation should be the first consideration in any communication plans. These requirements include defining the goals, expectations, and capabilities of the users of the communication system, including physicians, staff, patients, vendors, and any other stakeholder group that may require access to the practice. The sophistication of the communication system is often dependent on the level of sophistication of the users. If some users, such as elderly patients, are not computer literate, it is important to provide multiple avenues for communication to ensure that these patients can access the services provided by the practice.

The primary goal of patients is to have access to a communication system that allows them to communicate with the physician and the support staff as appropriate. Patients need to be able to make and change appointments, ask questions, obtain prescription renewals and referrals, request records, and discuss myriad other issues that are extremely important to the patient. Physicians and practice staff want a system by which they can communicate among themselves and with other health care providers and organizations, respond to patient requests, and attend to the normal business activities of an organization – and to do it all in an efficient and cost-effective manner.

The most obvious methods of communication include telephone, voice mail, fax, Internet, e-mail, pagers, and point-to-point delivery as serviced by the U.S. Postal Service, FedEx, UPS, and others. Each form of communication has its own purpose, which is normally derived from its individual strengths and weaknesses.

The most obvious and prevalent communication tool in use in practices is the telephone with voice mail capability. The strengths of the telephone lie primarily in its accessibility and its familiarity among all possible users. The telephone affords the user the opportunity to easily obtain live access to the target party. In the event that the desired recipient of the telephone communication is unavailable, the voice mail capability functions as an adequate, low-cost method of allowing the caller to leave messages for the recipient. The telephone system is limited only by the number of trunk lines that are installed and the number of personnel available to answer the calls. In addition, the telephone can act as a marketing tool, providing information concerning the practice through a message-on-hold program that provides information concerning the practice. This message does need to be updated on a regular basis, such as every three to six months, to keep it from becoming stale and annoying to those individuals who call the practice on a regular basis. After normal office hours, the telephone can be forwarded to any number of answering services who can function as the physician's office in taking and forwarding the appropriate messages and calls to the on-call physician, thereby ensuring a patient's twenty-four-hour access to medical support.

The weaknesses of this form of communication may, in some cases, seem contradictory to its strengths. Proper, detailed planning is again the best route to take to avoid or mitigate many of the weaknesses of a telephone system. This planning may include the use of call centers to receive and direct calls; defining call flow, including the use of hunt groups (a series of telephone lines identified as a group such that if one line is busy, the next available line is used – it "hunts" for the next line) and triage systems for handling inbound calls; developing answering standards; and handling emergency call protocols. Frustration among all of the users of the system will occur when a telephone system is not designed properly, resulting in calls that are not routed to the appropriate staff member, or when there are insufficient trunks to respond to the demand for access. Even where sufficient trunks exist, the lack of adequate numbers of properly trained staff to answer and respond to the volume of calls will also cause significant issues. Many users of telephone systems are intolerant of voice mail systems and are frustrated when calls are not returned on a timely basis. To reduce complaints concerning the use of voice mail systems, a practice needs to develop and implement detailed guidelines concerning expectations with regard to clearing and responding to voice mail messages. The use of auto-attendant and voice mail systems can become extremely confusing, especially for the elderly patient.

A relatively new communication tool being used by practices is through the development and implementation of Internet-based Websites and e-mail access. Through these sites, a practice can make its information available to a public made up of potential patients. Properly designed and publicized Websites also have the capability of reducing the volume of telephone calls received by an office by enabling existing patients to refill pharmaceuticals, request chart copies, download forms, obtain directions, and ask questions via e-mail. In addition to providing practice-specific information, Websites can provide medical education as well as links to other Websites concerning medical conditions and procedures that would otherwise result in telephone calls or extended office visits. Through the use of interactive programs located on a practice's Website, patients can become educated on surgical procedures being considered and the different types of clinical tests that the patient may receive. As this form of education can be accomplished at the patient's convenience, with respect to both time and location, it is a positive adjunct to the use of pamphlets, videotapes, and CDs. To be most effective, the Website should contain current, accurate information and be easy for the user to navigate (see Exhibit 3 for an example).

EXHIBIT 3.

Example of using a Website to educate patients

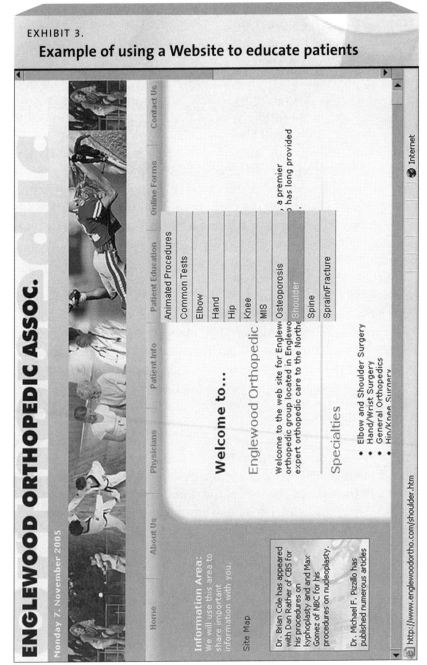

© 2005 Englewood Orthopedic Associates. Reprinted with permission.

The use of the Internet also allows a practice to respond to and handle other clinical and administrative functions, including obtaining clinical information from such other providers as hospitals and imaging centers as well as making use of available telemedicine services, if appropriate, based on geographic location. The various administrative functions that can be accomplished through the use of the Internet include electronic submission of insurance claims, confirmation of a patient's insurance coverage, follow-up on previously submitted insurance claims, and Web-based conferencing. To accomplish these tasks, sufficient bandwidth and data ports should be available to the staff and physicians who would utilize these services.

To effectively use the technical methods of communication, it is the responsibility of the practice to ensure that all staff receives proper training in the utilization of these tools. Staff and physicians should receive sufficient training to become proficient and comfortable in the use of all of the software and technological tools that assist them in the performance of their duties. As new technologies (e.g., EHRs, intra-office e-mail, and automated patient notification systems) are introduced into the practice, the need to train affected personnel in areas of data and word processing increases. Some of the training in specific technology applications may require formal training sessions, whereas other modalities, such as reading manuals and online training, may also be utilized. Even after initial training takes place, policies should be established to ensure that periodic refresher training is provided so individual staff members remain proficient and up-to-date on the specifics of the technology tools they are using. In addition, as previously discussed, the Internet is an extremely powerful avenue to provide educational opportunities to patients through the use of interactive educational programs that can either reside on a practice's Website or be accessed through links to other medical educational sites on the Web.

Most physicians carry personal cell phones, but many still use pagers or cell phone/pagers to enable the office or answering service to reach them when they are not in the office. Although pagers can be effective in notifying a physician that he or she is needed, they are limited in that they do not allow for two-way communication. The physician or other recipient of the page may be required to call or otherwise respond to the page to confirm that the page has been received.

The two remaining methods of communication are the use of fax transmissions and door-to-door delivery, such as normal postal mail, otherwise known as "snail mail." While neither method is used to any great extent to communicate with patients, both methods are used for physicians and other health care providers (e.g., hospitals, clinical laboratories, and imaging centers) to transfer needed patient information in a secure manner. As with all other methods of communication, policies need to be developed that determine how mail and other packages are to be handled when reaching the practice but not the specific intended recipient. An example of this would be whether physicians opened their own mail, or a member of the staff opened the mail and forwarded to the physician only the items that required the physician's attention.

The constant growth and evolution within the field of communication have resulted in easier methods of contact among patients, physicians, and other health care providers. Medical practices and their leadership should continue to embrace this growth in technology to ensure continued, effective communication between patients and the medical practices.

Develop Clinical Pathway Structure and Function

CLINICAL PATHWAYS are described as multidisciplinary plans of treatment that are developed to enable the implementation of clinical guidelines and protocols. While best known as clinical pathways, several other terms are used to describe this concept, including care maps, integrated care pathways, and collaborative care pathways. Clinical pathways are utilized to support clinical, resource, and financial management of a patient with a specific condition over a specified time period. The four major components to the clinical pathway include (1) a time line, (2) the type of care, (3) the outcome criteria, and (4) the variance record for identifying deviations from the norms and/or expectations.[8]

The goal of developing and implementing clinical pathways and clinical protocols is to attain a high level of quality of medical care by identifying, implementing, and adhering to specific medical standards by all physicians in a given specialty when treating a specific set of symptoms or identified illness or injury. Through the application of clinical pathways in the utilization of clinical protocols, a group practice will have the tools to generate clinical data that will enable the organization to prove to outside entities the level of clinical quality being provided by the practice.

Clinical pathways and protocols can be derived from multiple sources, including third-party payers, medical specialty societies, and the National Institutes of Health. Even though applying these protocols constitutes good clinical care on its own, the utilization of audits and external assessments to measure compliance with the protocols can be effectively used to confirm the quality of care being provided and therefore justify the negotiation of better contracts with third-party payers and improved relationships with local employers where direct contracting for medical services may be possible.

The effective development and implementation of clinical pathways within an organization requires a multidisciplinary approach, with input from all levels of clinical providers as well as input from nonclinical staff. The initial creation of this type of structure requires the full and unreserved endorsement and support of physicians as well as clinical and executive leadership of the organization. Preliminary meetings and discussions need to be held within the leadership structure to identify the organization-specific goals for the implementation of clinical pathways. In some cases, this may require the inclusion of various community collaborators who have involvement or responsibility for part of the care and treatment plan of the patient. Examples of this outside collaboration may include visiting-nurse services, rehabilitation facilities, and social services support agencies. In addition to being part of the leadership, administrative support goes further in the form of being advocates, facilitators, and champions to show that the organization is in favor of and supportive of the implementation of clinical pathways through both words and the identification and application of necessary financial and operational resources.

In addition, the development and implementation of clinical pathways may have significant effects that go beyond the simple goal of quality care. The development and application of clinical pathway structures, when properly communicated to staff, patients, and community stakeholders, send a clear and effective message that the practice is committed to maintaining services at no less than industry norms and is effective at both identifying and measuring those norms for improved patient care. Properly designed and implemented clinical pathways will also affect the cost of care through changes in the services that will be rendered based upon specific presented symptoms, and may have significant impact on insurance carrier–directed pay-for-performance models. The application of clinical pathways should also increase financial accountability through the elimination of redundancy and variations of clinical methods used by different providers.

In addition to developing and implementing this clinical pathway structure, an organization should create and implement a variety of quality assurance programs to measure the results of the implementation of the clinical pathways and ensure that the desired goals are being reached. The majority of quality assurance programs can be sized to meet the needs of both large and small medical practices. Dependent upon the size of the organization, some practices complete their quality assurance programs internally whereas other practices utilize outside consultants to complete the necessary reviews, audits, and surveys.

A key tool in evaluating adherence to clinical pathways and their effect on the patient population is through the use of various outcomes measures, including chart reviews, whereby a sample of medical records is reviewed to confirm that the proper care is being provided and properly documented in the medical record. Other measurements that can be used include patient and referring-physician satisfaction surveys. These surveys, when completed properly and analyzed in a timely manner, can provide a wealth of information concerning how well the clinical pathways are being received and whether the pathways are in keeping with the standards in the community and the expectations of the patient. The results of these reviews and surveys should be presented to senior clinical and administrative management to enable them to address the issues raised by the results of the surveys and reviews. The data used to define the issues may be perceived differently when reviewed by clinical and administrative staff. Clinicians will be primarily seeking to improve the care being provided to enable the patient to reach the best possible outcome. This goal is important from the administrative point of review as well, but the medical practice administrator is also concerned that the care and service are being provided in the most cost-effective manner with the most efficient use of available resources. Finally, these data are critical to identifying and determining modifications that need to be made in both the strategic and operational planning processes.

TASK 9 **Create Monitoring Systems for Licensure, Credentialing, and Recertification**

IN THE PERCEPTION OF THE PUBLIC, the primary reason for accreditation and credentialing is to be able to show that an outside, independent body has determined that an organization (or an individual) has been tested and has met standards that prove its level of quality and/or competency within the health care field. With regard to organizations and facilities, the primary accrediting bodies are the Joint Commission on Accreditation of Healthcare Organizations (JCAHO) and the Accreditation Association for Ambulatory Health Care (AAAHC). When pursuing accreditation, a practice or health care facility should undergo a rigorous multiday evaluation that addresses all aspects of the operation of the organization and the medical treatment that is being provided. Within this accreditation process, an organization can expect that evaluations of the following areas will take place: governing by-laws, safety and health procedures, facility design and safety, chart documentation, human resources, quality assurance reviews, and physician and staff credentialing. In addition, the development, implementation, and adherence to documented policies and procedures that delineate and govern the day-to-day operations of the practice are critical to the successful completion of the accreditation process. This in-depth evaluation is repeated, normally on a three-year cycle, to ensure that the findings of both the initial and subsequent evaluations are still within the expected values that earned the organization its original accreditation. Failure to meet the expected standards places a requirement on the organization to implement corrective action to address those issues that did not meet the standards of the accrediting body. Continued failure to be responsive to and correct these deficiencies can result in increasing levels of response from the accrediting body, with the ultimate response being the revocation of the certificate of accreditation.

In addition to these accreditation organizations, other recognized professional organizations provide the means to credential or certify the competency of physicians and administrators. Physicians obtain their board certification through the completion of specialty training and the successful passing of comprehensive examinations that test their knowledge and expertise within their defined areas of specialization. In many cases, this board certification is required to obtain privileges within hospital staffs and participation on various insurance carrier provider panels. This board certification is specialty-controlled, and retaining this certification normally requires that the physician complete specified numbers of continuing-education credits each year as well as take periodic re-examinations intended to ensure that the physician has remained current with the changes in the field of specialty.

This form of comprehensive testing also is available to health care administrators as a means of confirming their expertise and ability in the field of health care management. The two organizations that are recognized for providing this testing and certification are the American College of Medical Practice Executives (ACMPE) and the American College of Healthcare Executives (ACHE). Whereas ACMPE's primary thrust is in the area of group practice management, ACHE is the more prevalent credentialing body in the area of hospital administration. Both organizations require that a member who has attained certification complete a specified number of continuing-education hours in each three-year period to retain the certification designation.

In addition to the professional credentialing organizations previously discussed, physicians are also credentialed by licensed health care facilities (e.g., hospitals and nursing homes) and by commercial and noncommercial insurance carriers. Each organization has its own policies and procedures for credentialing providers and confirming and updating those credentials. Each entity has its own regulations that must be followed by the credentialed provider. In the event of noncompliance with the policies and guidelines of the credentialing body, the provider may be subject to progressive disciplinary action, which ultimately may result in the provider losing credentialed status with the entity. Normally, the provider is advised of the area of noncompliance and is offered the opportunity to implement corrective action within a defined period of time. Failure to implement corrective action or continued violations of the specific policies and procedures may result in progressively stronger disciplinary actions including suspension and ultimate termination from the staff, if a health care facility, or termination from the provider panel, if an insurance carrier.

To properly and effectively manage the myriad regulations, licenses, and credentialing requirements of its health care providers, it is advantageous for the practice to develop a database that reflects and summarizes all of these areas so that the practice's leadership can, at a glance, identify areas of conflict or areas where information requires updating. A simple way to create such a database is through the use of electronic spreadsheets, which can be updated as information on the individual members of the practice changes. Through the use of spreadsheets, a practice can chart the status of the credentialing of individual providers within a health plan, and can maintain an electronic "tickler file" of when various licenses and certifications are due for renewal.

TASK 10　**Develop and Implement Process Improvement Programs for Clinic Operations**

GROWTH, CHANGE, AND EVOLUTION constitute the goal and the reason to develop and implement process improvement programs within a practice. The practice that does not constantly test its own organization's core processes and develop and implement ways to improve the operation will not evolve but will stagnate and eventually be unable to meet the clinical and business challenges of the future.

Process improvement means challenging "the way that things have always been done." Not all process improvement programs will succeed in meeting their goals, but all will produce a positive gain for the organization that is willing to take some risk to improve themselves. Through the use of audits, outside reviews, compliance reviews, and just standing back and asking "Why do we do this process this way?" an organization can identify the key areas where improvements in the operation and life of the practice can be made. Process improvement also requires investment – investment in time and thought to evaluate a system and determine a better way to do the job, and investment in education, for it is through education that leadership for improvement is born.

In the realm of clinical practice, areas for review that may result in process improvement include coding documentation, risk assessments, chart audits, and auditing of compliance with regulatory and payer regulations. Within these areas, specific types of audits, reviews, and assessments can include:

1. Reviewing medical records to evaluate completeness of documentation and to identify those providers whose documentation either does not support the procedural code used or who are using a procedural code that is lower than the documentation can support;

2. Compare the compliance requirements of the various regulatory agencies and third-party payers that use guidelines and policies to ensure the practice meets the expectations of these outside entities; and

3. Reviewing and analyzing the historical data of the organization (e.g., malpractice claims, patient complaints, and external evaluations) to identify trends and areas for additional review and analysis.

All of these reviews can be used as part of larger outcome-based quality assurance programs, which in turn give rise to and support many process improvement initiatives. The vital components of a quality assurance program are structure, process, and outcome, which constitute the framework for quality assurance activities and provide the operational focus for them. Clearly, no one method of measurement has yet evolved as a sole standard of measurement.[9] In most cases, these areas are first addressed through the use of the various audits and assessments. Within larger organizations, these audits can be done internally, assuming qualified personnel exist within the practice; in other cases, these reviews can be contracted out to qualified consultants who can provide the same data at low cost to the practice.

The findings, which reflect on the current structure, process, and outcomes of the services of the organization, are often presented to senior clinical and administrative management for review and corrective action. Without proper and effective communication to all stakeholders, the value of these findings is greatly diminished. To be most effective, communication of these findings should be provided in written format, but within the context of a face-to-face meeting where effective discussion can take place.

These findings, if utilized properly, become the basis for implementing the various methodologies that may be applied to improve the processes within the organization, including:

1. Flowcharting the process being reviewed, as shown in Exhibit 2, to identify possible redundancies or blockages within the process;

2. Reviewing historical data that may exist from previous assessments, such as chart audits, coding reviews, and risk assessments, and comparing those data to current data to identify variations and possible trends that will spotlight concerns and issues; and

3. Completing surveys of patient, referring physician, and employee satisfaction levels to identify issues of concern to these groups of stakeholders.

These methodologies are useful in identifying issues, areas for improvement, and possible systemic changes to the processes in effect. It is often advisable to test the changes through the use of pilot programs before implementing the changes on an organization-wide basis. Through application on a limited scale, an organization is able to test the proposed changes to ensure that there are no unanticipated ramifications emanating from them. Once these changes are proven through a pilot program, they can be applied safely throughout the organization.

In order to properly apply and maximize the effect of these reviews within the organization, it is necessary to create teaching models and techniques that effectively impart this knowledge to the staff of the organization. These models vary significantly, based upon several factors, including the size of the organization, the staff mix that exists, the complexity of the changes that are being envisioned, and the amount of time that can be made available for training and education purposes. In small organizations, this training can consist of staff meetings, with senior physicians and management providing the training through the use of lectures and roundtable discussions. In larger practices, this training and education may be expanded to include department-specific classes, use of online training programs, and sending staff members to off-site courses and seminars. Without this training and support from senior management and physicians, it is very difficult, if not impossible, to obtain staff buy-in to these new process improvements. It is through this investment in time and resources that an organization will be able to realize improvements in their processes and their clinical outcomes.

Conclusion

THIS VOLUME has touched on the skill sets needed to become adept in accomplishing the tasks within the Business and Clinical Operations domain within the *ACMPE Guide to the Body of Knowledge for Medical Practice Management*. The information provided should assist the medical practice administrator in addressing and responding to the ongoing operational and clinical demands of his or her practice.

It is important to remember that to maximize the effectiveness of these skill sets, they should be kept within the context and understanding of the basic principles of all of the five general competencies:

1. Professionalism;

2. Leadership;

3. Communication Skills;

4. Organizational and Analytical Skills; and

5. Technical/Professional Knowledge and Skills.

Without the knowledge that can be obtained from a full understanding of all competencies within the *Guide*, it will be difficult to properly apply the knowledge that is obtained from any one competency or skill.

Exercises

THESE QUESTIONS have been retired from the ACMPE Essay Exam question bank. Because there are so many ways to handle various situations, there are no "right" answers, and thus, no answer key. Use these questions to help you practice responses in different scenarios.

1. You are an administrator of a medical group practice. A patient presents to the clinic and states that she has an appointment. The receptionist checks the schedule and does not find an appointment for this patient. The patient insists she was given the appointment time and has a reminder card at home to prove she is accurate. The receptionist states that the doctor already has a full schedule for the morning. The patient is upset and demands to be seen.

Describe how would you handle this situation.

2. A surgeon in your practice performed a medically necessary
    and successful surgery on a patient. Your practice is known
    for its excellent patient satisfaction and tries in every way
    to resolve issues to the patient's satisfaction. Your office
    staff failed to pre-certify the surgery, and the patient's
    insurance company refuses to pay the hospital bill. The
    patient, stating that your office assured her that they
    would handle the pre-certification, now insists that the
    practice should "take care of" the hospital bill or she
    will sue.

    What course of action would you take in this situation?

3. You are an administrator of a large multispecialty medical
    group practice. During the past 24 months, there has been
    a drop in work relative value units (RVUs) for physicians
    and other providers. In two weeks, there is a meeting of the
    executive committee, and you have been asked to
    specifically identify the factors that have contributed to the
    decline and estimate what the impact has been on the
    medical group.

    What course of action would you take in this situation?

4. You are the administrator of a 40-physician multispecialty medical group with several locations. Each clinic is responsible for ordering, maintaining, and distributing patient care supplies, including pharmaceuticals. Each of these locations also has extensive supplies of sample medications. Your new director of nursing has reported missing pharmaceuticals and sample medications from at least two different locations during the past week. Her initial investigation reveals that there are no written policies or formal inventory control processes in place.

   What course of action would you take in this situation?

5. You are the administrator of a 10-physician surgical group. A major insurer from which you receive 30 percent of your total revenue has announced that it will reduce reimbursement rates by an average of 25 percent within the next 60 days. You have been instructed by your board of directors to cut your overhead expenses by 10 percent and to ensure that the physicians' distributed compensation does not significantly decrease. The physicians want you to report back to them on how you are going to cut expenses at the next board meeting (in two weeks).

   What course of action would you take in this situation?

6. You are the administrator of a 20-physician multispecialty medical group with four locations. The group was created two years ago by the merger of three existing practices. Several of the physicians practice at multiple sites. Each of the four sites has its own medical records format and methods of documenting patient care. A recent internal audit revealed inconsistencies in medical record documentation across the various sites. The deficiencies include illegible notes, inconsistent use of abbreviations, and a lack of sufficient documentation of care and courses of treatment. Several physicians have commented that it is difficult to work with multiple chart formats.

What course of action would you take in this situation?

7. You are the new chief operating officer of a large multispecialty group with a number of locations. As chief operating officer, you report to the executive board and are administratively responsible for all business operations. In your first week on the job, the business manager asks to schedule an appointment with you. The business manager reports that one of the locations is having trouble getting its daily postings completed. Charges are not being entered in a timely manner, bank deposits are made sporadically, demographic information is not regularly updated, and coding errors are frequent. In the course of the conversation, you discover that all offices have similar problems and are making little effort to correct the processes, even though they have been notified repeatedly by the business manager about the issues.

What course of action would you take in this situation?

8. You are the new chief executive officer of a large group practice. Managed-care penetration has driven reimbursement down and increased administrative support services. Your group has been approached by a large hospital system that wants to buy your practice and employ your physicians. A smaller specialty group has suggested a merger to strengthen your market position. Several of your tenured stockholders are resistant to considering these changes. The health care system's offer expires in 90 days, The president of the board has asked you to present your recommendations at a special board meeting.

What course of action would you take in this situation?

Notes

1. Austin Ross, Stephen J. Williams, & Ernest J. Pavlock, *Ambulatory Care Management* (Englewood, Colo.: Medical Group Management Association, 1998), 72.

2. Albert Barnett & Gloria Gilbert Mayer, *Ambulatory Care Management and Practice* (Gaithersburg, Md.: Aspen Publishers, 1992), 39–41.

3. Ross, Williams, & Pavlock, *Ambulatory Care Management*, 196.

4. David Gans, "Squeezed? Think Ancillary Services," *MGMA Connexion* 3, no. 2 (2003): 25.

5. Brian Mathwich, MD, "Using the Process Map to Improve Your Bottom Line," *MGMA Connexion* 4, no. 6 (2004): 31.

6. Elizabeth Woodcock, *Mastering Patient Flow* (Englewood, Colo.: Medical Group Management Association, 2003), 88.

7. Ross, Williams, & Pavlock, *Ambulatory Care Management*, 196.

8. "Clinical Pathways," www.openclinical.org/clinicalpathways.html (retrieved October 13, 2005).

9. Barnett & Mayer, *Ambulatory Care Management and Practice*, 291.

About the Author

Edward Gulko, MBA, FACMPE, CHE, is the administrator of Orthopedic Associates of Englewood, located in Englewood, New Jersey. He has previously held senior positions with other group practices as well as senior hospital administration roles within the New York City Health and Hospitals Corporation.

Mr. Gulko has served on various committees of both MGMA and ACMPE. He is currently serving as president of the MGMA New Jersey chapter and is the New Jersey state director of the American Academy of Medical Administrators (AAMA).

Mr. Gulko received a bachelor of science degree in Industrial Engineering from the New Jersey Institute of Technology and a master of business administration degree in Health Administration from Temple University. He is a fellow of ACMPE and a diplomate in the American College of Healthcare Executives (ACHE). He is also currently licensed in the state of New Jersey as a nursing home administrator.

In January 2004, Mr. Gulko retired from the U.S. Navy Reserve with the rank of Lieutenant Commander, Medical Service Corps. His service included assignments in support units of the Bureau of Medicine and Surgery, National Naval Medical Center – Bethesda, U.S. Central Command, and 4th Marine Division. Mr. Gulko also served on active duty during Operation Desert Storm, and as a field interviewer for students seeking admission to the United States Naval Academy.

Index

Accreditation Association for
    Ambulatory Health Care
    (AAAHC), 59
American College of Healthcare
    Executives (ACHE), 60,
    79
American College of Medical
    Practice Executives
    (ACMPE)
    essay exam, 69
    Guide, xi, 67
Americans with Disablities Act
    of 1990 (ADA), 14, 38
Ambulatory
    care management, 77
    health care, 59
Ancillary services, 14, 22, 24,
    25-29
Appointment, 23, 34, 41-44,
    47, 69, 75

Business operations planning,
    13, 17-19

Charges, 3, 27, 41, 48, 75
Clinical
    operations, 9, 16, 63, 65
    issues, 9
    tasks, 13, 15
    pathways, 7, 15, 55-57
    support services, 14, 25-29
Clinical Laboratory
    Improvement Act (CLIA),
    28
Co-pay, 42-43, 48
Communicating, 12, 45, 48
Communication skills, 6, 67
Cost Survey, 21, 27
Create monitoring systems, 16,
    59, 61
Credentialing, 16, 28, 59-61

Electronic health record (EHR),
    47, 53
Ethics committee, 8

Facilities planning, 14, 37-39
Financial management, 7, 55
Flowcharting, 65

General competencies, 5-8, 67
Governance, 6, 8

Health Insurance Portability
    and Accountability Act
    (HIPAA), 10, 29, 34, 47-
    48
Human resource management,
    8, 24

Information management, 8,
    10, 29, 67
Insurance, 23, 25, 43, 45, 46,
    47, 48, 53, 57, 60, 61, 70
Internet, 50, 53
Inventory control systems, 14,
    31, 33, 35

Joint Commission on
    Accreditation of
    Healthcare Organizations
    (JCAHO), 59

Knowledge needs, 11-12

Leadership, 6, 8, 19, 54, 56, 61,
    64, 67
Licensure, 16, 28, 59, 61

Maintenance programs, 14, 37-
    40
Marketing, 7, 50
Medicaid, 45
Medical Group Management
    Association (MGMA), 27,
    42-43
Medicare, 45
Mission statement, 17-18
Monitoring systems, 14, 59-61